The Emotional Intelligence Edge

The Emotional Intelligence Edge

MASTERING THE ART OF RELATIONSHIPS

Carmen Wilde

QuantumQuill Press

Contents

1

Chapter 1: Introduction to Emotional Intelligence

Characterizing The capacity to understand individuals on a deeper level:

The capacity to understand people on a deeper level (EI) fills in as the foundation of our cooperation, both with ourselves and with others. At its substance, EI epitomizes the capacity to perceive, comprehend, and deal with our own feelings, as well as to understand the feelings of everyone around us. It is the establishment whereupon we construct solid connections, explore testing circumstances, and, at last, track down satisfaction in our lives.

In this part, we set out on an excursion to unwind the multifaceted layers of the capacity to understand people on a deeper level. We dig into its diverse nature, taking apart the center parts that comprise this priceless range of abilities. From the profundities of mindfulness to the levels of social adroitness, we investigate how every aspect of EI adds to our general close-to-home sharpness.

By characterizing the ability to understand people on a deeper level in clear and substantial terms, we lay the foundation for the groundbreaking investigation that lies ahead. Together, we set out on a journey to excel at connections from the perspective of the capacity to understand people on a deeper level, furnishing ourselves with the devices and experiences important to flourish in an undeniably interconnected world.

The advancement of the capacity to understand anyone on a profound level:

All through the chronicles of mankind's set of experiences, the idea of the capacity to understand individuals on a profound level has gone through a striking development, reflecting the moving tides of cultural qualities and logical requests. From the old insight of scholars to the historic examination of current clinicians, the excursion of EI is one set apart by significant bits of knowledge and perspective changes.

In this part, we follow the ancestry of the ability to understand people on a deeper level, enlightening its way from lack of definition to conspicuousness on the worldwide stage. We venture through the passages of time, investigating crucial minutes and persuasive figures who formed how we might interpret feelings and their significant effect on human behavior.

From the spearheading work of Daniel Goleman to the original hypotheses of Howard Gardner, we witness the assembly of dissimilar disciplines in the mission to disentangle the secrets of the human mind. We uncover how EI rose up out of the shadows of the scholarly world to turn into a directing guide in fields as different as schooling, administration, and psychological well-being.

As we consider the development of the capacity to understand people on a profound level, we gain a more profound appreciation for its perseverance through pertinence in a steadily impacting world. Outfitted with verifiable experiences and newly discovered lucidity, we set up for a more profound investigation of EI's logical underpinnings and pragmatic applications in the parts that follow.

The science behind the ability to understand individuals on a profound level:

Inside the complex maze of the human mind lie the organic

underpinnings of our feelings, directing our considerations, activities, and connections. In this section, we set out on a journey into the domain of neuroscience, where we uncover the entrancing transaction between science and feeling that shapes the bedrock of the capacity to understand people on a profound level.

Drawing after state-of-the art examination and momentous disclosures, we enlighten the brain circuits that administer our close-to-home reactions and shape our impression of the world. From the amygdala's job as the sentinel of risk to the prefrontal cortex's ability for sane ideas, we disentangle the perplexing embroidered artwork of the mind's personal design.

From the perspective of logical request, we investigate how feelings are not simple vaporous states yet strong powers that shape our world and impact our independent direction. We dive into the components of a close-to-home guideline, uncovering systems to saddle the force of our feelings and develop more noteworthy versatility even with difficulty.

As we strip back the layers of the cerebrum's personal scene, we gain a more profound comprehension of our own internal operations and the significant ramifications for our connections and prosperity. Equipped with newly discovered experiences into the science behind capacity to understand people on a deeper level, we set out on an excursion of self-revelation and change, prepared to open our maximum capacity in the sections that lie ahead.

Surveying your ability to understand people on a profound level:

Setting out on the way to dominating capacity to understand people on a deeper level requires a sharp identity mindfulness and a fair examination of our assets and shortcomings in exploring the many-sided landscape of human feelings. In this section, we set out on an excursion of reflection, directed by devices and methods intended to enlighten the shapes of our profound scene.

We start by disentangling the unpredictable strings of our deepest contemplations and sentiments, looking into the profundities of our awareness to observe the examples that shape our close-to-home reactions. Through intelligent activities and self-appraisal apparatuses, we gain clarity on our profound assets and regions for development, laying the basis for significant change and self-improvement.

As we explore the territory of self-disclosure, we come up against the horde of impacts that shape our profound reality, from youth encounters to cultural standards and social assumptions. With every disclosure, we inch closer to a more profound comprehension of ourselves and the significant effect our feelings have on our connections and, by and large, prosperity.

Furnished with newly discovered bits of knowledge and our capacity to understand individuals on a deeper level, we stand balanced on the limit of change, prepared to leave on an excursion of development and discipline. With fortitude and responsibility, we embrace the difficulties and valuable open doors that lie ahead, realizing that the way to a more prominent capacity to understand people on a deeper level starts with a solitary step of mindfulness.

The Advantages of Creating the Ability to Understand Anyone on a Profound Level:

As we venture further into the domains of the capacity to understand people on a profound level, we uncover an abundance of remunerations anticipating the individuals who try to step this ground-breaking way. In this section, we investigate the bunch of benefits that emerge from sharpening our close-to-home keenness, advancing our own connections, and opening new vistas of expert achievement.

At the core of the capacity to appreciate individuals on a profound level lies the capacity to produce further associations with others, to understand their encounters and points of view, and to speak with lucidity and sympathy. By developing these abilities, we support obligations of trust and shared regard that structure the groundwork of sound, satisfying connections.

Also, the advantages of the capacity to appreciate individuals on a deeper level stretch out a long way beyond the bounds of our own lives, saturating each part of our expert undertakings. From rousing groups to arrive at new levels of cooperation and advancement to exploring the intricacies of authority with beauty and honesty, EI enables us to flourish in the high-speed, interconnected universe of the 21st century.

Yet, maybe the best compensation of all lies in the domain of discipline, in the significant feeling of satisfaction that emerges from knowing ourselves profoundly and legitimately. As we embrace the excursion of fostering our capacity to understand people on a profound level, we open the way to an existence of more noteworthy versatility, satisfaction, and reason—aa day-to-day existence directed by the insight of the heart and the clarity of the brain.

2

Chapter 2: Cultivating Self-Awareness

Grasping the Significance of Mindfulness:

In the maze of human experience, mindfulness remains a directing reference point, enlightening the forms of our internal scene with lucidity and knowledge. It is the foundation whereupon the ability to understand anyone on a profound level is constructed, engaging us to explore the intricacies of our feelings, considerations, and ways of behaving with beauty and credibility.

In this part, we set out on an excursion to unwind the significant meaning of mindfulness in the journey for self-improvement and satisfaction. We investigate how mindfulness fills in as a mirror, reflecting back to us the insights of our reality—our longings, fears, assets, and weaknesses.

From the perspective of mindfulness, we gain a more profound comprehension of the perplexing transaction between our inward world and the outside powers that shape our existence. We figure out how to perceive the inconspicuous subtleties of our feelings, the examples of our viewpoints, and the inspirations driving our activities, making us ready for more prominent lucidity and discipline.

As we dig into the profundities of mindfulness, we come to

understand that it isn't just an objective yet a long-lasting excursion—an excursion of investigation, disclosure, and development. Furnished with the insight gathered from this section, we leave on the way to developing a more significant and genuine connection with ourselves, realizing that mindfulness is the way to opening the door to the completion of our human potential.

The Way to Self-Disclosure:

Leaving on the excursion of self-disclosure is much the same as heading out on an odyssey of the spirit—aa journey of investigation into the profundities of our being, directed by the compass of mindfulness. In this part, we set out on this extraordinary mission, charting a course through the huge span of our inward scene, looking for truth, importance, and realness.

At the core of self-revelation lies the act of care—an old workmanship that welcomes us to secure our mindfulness right now, to notice our contemplations and feelings with interest and non-judgment. Through care, we develop the ability to observe the recurring pattern of our internal experience and to recognize the inconspicuous murmurs of our instincts in the midst of the commotion of our day-to-day existence.

Notwithstanding care, we investigate different practices that work with self-disclosure, for example, journaling, contemplation, and self-reflection. Through the demonstration of composing, we give voice to the deepest openings of our spirit, uncovering stowed-away insights and uncovering hidden fortunes of understanding and shrewdness.

As we navigate the territory of self-revelation, we might experience deterrents and difficulties enroute—question, dread, opposition. However, it is through these very challenges that we develop and advance, becoming more grounded, smarter, and stronger than previously.

Eventually, the way to self-disclosure is a profoundly private excursion that is interesting to every person. However, it is an excursion that we don't embrace alone. With fortitude, interest, and sympathy as our directing colleagues, we set out on this sacrosanct journey, realizing that the objective isn't a spot, but a condition—aa condition of significant mindfulness and self-acknowledgment that holds the way into our most profound satisfaction and freedom.

Defeating Boundaries to Mindfulness:

Chasing mindfulness, we frequently experience imposing hindrances that discourage our way, creating shaded areas upon the radiance of our internal truth. In this section, we go up against these impediments head-on, furnished with mental fortitude, flexibility, and a steady purpose to develop how we might interpret ourselves.

One of the most widely recognized boundaries of mindfulness is forswearing—the refusal to recognize parts of ourselves that are awkward or badly arranged. Whether it be unsettled injury, imbued examples of conduct, or profoundly held convictions, refusal raises walls around our cognizance, safeguarding us from the excruciating bits of insight that lie underneath the surface. However, it is only by stripping back these layers of refusal that we can really see ourselves as we are, unfiltered and unadorned.

One more obstruction to mindfulness is evasion—the inclination to occupy ourselves with awkward feelings or troublesome bits of insight through hecticness, idealism, or desensitizing ways of behaving. By desensitizing ourselves to torment, we may briefly lighten our distress, yet in doing so, we likewise dull our ability for development and change. To conquer aversion, we should have the mental fortitude to incline toward inconvenience, to sit with our feelings without judgment or obstruction, and to embrace the full range of our human experience.

At long last, self-analysis can act as an impressive boundary to mindfulness, sustaining a pattern of disgrace, responsibility, and self-question that mists our view of ourselves. To break free from this cycle, we should develop self-empathy—the act of treating ourselves with graciousness, understanding, and pardoning, particularly in moments of battle or disappointment.

As we explore the misleading territory of mindfulness, we might stagger and waver enroute. However, it is through these very battles that we develop and advance, becoming more grounded, smarter, and stronger than previously. With every hindrance we survive, we draw one stage closer to the significant mindfulness and self-acknowledgment that lie at the core of our excursion.

Embracing Weakness:

In the embroidery of human experience, weakness is often apparent as an indication of shortcoming—aa delicate string to be stowed away, safeguarded from the cruel look of judgment and examination. However, in the excursion of mindfulness, we come to comprehend that weakness isn't an obligation yet a wellspring of significant strength and fortitude—an entryway to more profound association, legitimacy, and development.

In this part, we investigate the extraordinary force of embracing weakness as an impetus for mindfulness and individual development. We discover that weakness isn't inseparable from shortcoming, but rather with legitimacy—the eagerness to appear, be completely seen, and be completely heard, even despite vulnerability and hazards.

Through weakness, we develop the mental fortitude to talk about our reality, to share our feelings of trepidation and uncertainty, and to recognize the pieces of ourselves that we might have long kept secret in the shadows. In doing so, we make space for recuperating, association, and development, producing further obligations of trust and closeness with ourselves as well as other people.

Besides, weakness permits us to embrace the full range of our human experience—the ups and downs, the delights and distresses, the victories and disappointments. By embracing weakness, we figure out how to incline toward distress, to embrace defect, and to track down strength in our common mankind.

As we venture further into the core of weakness, we come to understand that it's anything but an indication of shortcoming yet an identification of legitimacy—aa demonstration of our eagerness to embrace the completion of our humankind. With each step we take on this excursion, we recover our power, our office, and our intrinsic value, realizing that genuine mindfulness starts with the mental fortitude to be helpless.

Incorporating mindfulness into day-to-day existence:

Mindfulness, while significant in its importance, finds its actual strength when coordinated into the texture of our regular routines. In this part, we investigate reasonable methodologies and strategies for meshing the embroidered artwork of mindfulness into the details of our schedules, propensities, and associations.

One strong method for integrating mindfulness into our day-to-day existence is through the act of care—an old craftsmanship that welcomes us to moor our mindfulness right now, to notice our contemplations, sentiments, and sensations with interest and non-judgment. By integrating care into exercises like eating, strolling, and, in any event, washing dishes, we develop a more profound association with ourselves and our general surroundings.

Journaling likewise fills in as a strong device for developing mindfulness, providing a place of refuge to investigate our deepest contemplations, sentiments, and encounters. Through the demonstration of composing, we gain lucidity on our qualities, needs, and objectives, uncovering bits of knowledge and disclosures that might have escaped us in the hecticness of day-to-day existence.

Moreover, we can integrate mindfulness into our associations with others by rehearsing undivided attention and sympathy—abilities that empower us to comprehend and interface with the encounters and points of view of people around us. By tuning into the feelings and signals of others, we extend our ability for sympathy and empathy, cultivating further and more significant connections.

Eventually, the way to integrating mindfulness into day-to-day existence lies in consistency, purposefulness, and self-empathy. By promising to develop mindfulness in all parts of our lives, we open the groundbreaking force of this significant work, introducing another period of development, credibility, and satisfaction.

3

Chapter 3: Mastering Self-Regulation

Grasping Self-Guideline:

In the mind-boggling dance of human feelings, self-guideline arises as a wonderful director, directing the ensemble of our inward encounters with balance and artfulness. In this part, we leave on an excursion to disentangle the significant meaning of self-guideline in the domain of the capacity to understand people on a profound level, investigating its basic standards and viable applications.

At its center, self-guideline envelops the capacity to oversee and regulate our feelings, driving forces, and responses as per our qualities, objectives, and conditions. It is the craft of bridling the crude energy of our feelings, directing them valuably, and keeping a feeling of equilibrium and harmony in the midst of life's unavoidable highs and lows.

From the perspective of self-guideline, we gain knowledge about the mind-boggling exchange between our viewpoints, feelings, and ways of behaving—the fragile environment that administers our inward world. We come to comprehend how self-guideline enables us to explore the wild flows of our feelings with beauty and flexibility, fashioning a pathway towards more prominent, profound prosperity and satisfaction.

Besides, self-guideline fills in as a key part in our associations with others, empowering us to impart successfully, resolve clashes helpfully, and develop further associations based on trust and common regard. By excelling at self-guideline, we become engineers of our own pre-determination, enabling us to profoundly impact our lives as per our most noteworthy desires and most profound qualities.

As we leave on this excursion of understanding self-guideline, we do so with a feeling of interest, receptiveness, and lowliness, realizing that the way to authority is cleared with persistence, practice, and self-reflection. With each step we follow along this way, we move closer to the extraordinary expectation that exists—the ability to direct our feelings, explore life's difficulties with flexibility, and live with more noteworthy realness and reason.

Figuring out self-guidance

In the multifaceted dance of human feelings, self-guideline arises as a mind-blowing director, directing the orchestra of our internal world with accuracy and beauty. At its center, self-guideline epitomizes the specialty of dealing with our driving forces, feelings, and ways of behaving in accordance with our qualities and objectives. In this part, we set out on an excursion to disentangle the significant meaning of self-guideline in the domain of the capacity to understand people on a deeper level.

From the perspective of self-guideline, we gain knowledge about the mind-boggling instruments that administer our profound reactions and responses. We come to comprehend how the capacity to adjust our motivations and control our close-to-home excitement is fundamental for exploring the intricacies of social communications, using wise judgment, and accomplishing our drawn-out desires.

Besides, self-guideline fills in as a foundation of profound versatility, engaging us to face the hardships of existence with composure and beauty. By developing the ability to control our feelings and ways of behaving, we pave the way towards more prominent discipline, flexibility, and prosperity.

As we dive further into the subtleties of self-guideline, we uncover commonsense methodologies and procedures for improving this fundamental ability. Through care rehearsals, mental social systems, and unwinding methods, we figure out how to develop more noteworthy mindfulness and command over our viewpoints, feelings, and activities, enabling us to explore life's difficulties with balance and certainty.

Eventually, the excursion of dominating self-guideline is one of significant self-disclosure and change—an excursion that engages us to bridle the maximum capacity of our ability to understand individuals on a deeper level and live with more noteworthy validness, reason, and flexibility.

The Study of Self-Guideline

Digging into the many-sided functions of the human cerebrum reveals the dazzling apparatus that supports our ability for self-guideline. In this part, we leave on an entrancing investigation of the neuroscience behind self-guideline, digging profoundly into the brain circuits and components that oversee our close-to-home reactions and driving forces.

At the core of self-guideline lies the prefrontal cortex, a district of the cerebrum entrusted with chief capabilities, for example, navigation, drive control, and profound guidance. Through the complicated transaction between the prefrontal cortex and subcortical locales like the amygdala and insula, our cerebrums organize a fragile harmony between profound reactivity and mental control.

As we dig further into the neuroscience of self-guideline, we reveal the significant ramifications for how we might interpret human ways of behaving and gain insight. We come to see the value in how disturbances in the brain's basic self-guideline can appear in a range of situations, from tension and gloom to compulsion and impulsivity.

Also, we investigate the unique exchange between brain adaptability and self-guideline, perceiving the mind's wonderful ability to adjust and change because of involvement and preparation. Through deliberate practice and reiteration, we can shape our brain processes, reinforcing the circuits that help self-guideline and debilitating those that sustain maladaptive examples of conduct.

Armed with a more profound comprehension of the neuroscience behind self-guideline, we are better prepared to develop this fundamental expertise and tackle its extraordinary power in our day-to-day routines. By utilizing the experiences gathered from neuroscience, we can open new roads for self-awareness, strength, and prosperity, making us ready for a more adjusted, satisfying, and amicable presence.

Procedures for Improving Self-Guidelines

In the many-sided embroidery of human experience, becoming amazing at self-guideline is likened to winding around sensitive strings of mindfulness, deliberateness, and discipline into the texture of our regular routines. In this section, we set out on an excursion of investigation, revealing pragmatic systems and strategies for upgrading our ability for self-guideline and profound equilibrium.

At the core of successful self-guideline lies the act of care—an old craftsmanship that welcomes us to secure our mindfulness right now, to notice our contemplations, feelings, and real sensations with interest and non-judgment. Through care practices like contemplation, breathwork, and body examinations, we develop more noteworthy attention to our inward scene, engaging us to answer life's difficulties with clarity and poise.

Furthermore, mental conduct procedures offer amazing assets for upgrading self-guideline by testing and reevaluating maladaptive ideas, examples, and ways of behaving. By distinguishing and supplanting negative self-talk with more versatile and engaging stories, we can change our internal exchange and develop a more sure and strong outlook.

In addition, unwinding methods like profound breathing, moderate muscle unwinding, and directed symbolism give priceless assets to lessening pressure, uneasiness, and close-to-home excitement. By integrating these practices into our day-to-day daily schedule, we can relieve our sensory system, reestablish harmony with our feelings, and develop a more noteworthy feeling of inward harmony and prosperity.

As we investigate these assorted techniques for improving self-guideline, we perceive that every individual might resonate with various methodologies. By trying different things with different strategies and finding what turns out best for us, we can fit our self-guideline practice to suit our extraordinary requirements, inclinations, and conditions.

At last, the excursion of dominating self-guideline is one of progressing investigation and refinement—an excursion that welcomes us to develop more prominent mindfulness, flexibility, and profound equilibrium in our lives. With devotion, diligence, and an open heart, we can bridle the groundbreaking force of self-guideline to explore life's difficulties with beauty, astuteness, and inward strength.

Defeating Normal Difficulties

Chasing dominating self-guidelines, we definitely experience a bunch of difficulties that test the versatility of our purpose and the profundity of our responsibility. In this section, we stand up to these hindrances head-on, outfitted with knowledge, empathy, and an unfaltering assurance to develop more prominent, profound equilibrium and discipline.

One normal test of self-guidance is the unavoidable presence of stress—aa pervasive power in our current lives that can overpower our ability to successfully deal with our feelings and motivations. Whether coming from work pressures, relationship clashes, or monetary concerns, stress can commandeer our sensory system, setting off a fountain of physiological and mental reactions that subvert our capacity to direct our feelings.

In addition, weakness and weariness can present huge boundaries to self-guideline, draining our mental assets and decreasing our ability for restraint and motivation. In snapshots of exhaustion, we might find ourselves more powerless due to hasty ways of behaving, profound reactivity, and dynamic blunders, making it difficult to remain grounded and focused in the midst of life's difficulties.

Moreover, outside triggers and allurements can wreck our endeavors to self-manage, enticing us to capitulate to old propensities and examples of conduct that never again serve our most noteworthy great. Whether it be the charm of undesirable food varieties, the temptation of computerized interruptions, or the draw of drugs, outer triggers can subvert our best goals and mislead us from our way of discipline.

However, even with these difficulties, we find ourselves stowing away supplies of solidarity, versatility, and assurance that empower us to drive forward and flourish. By developing more noteworthy mindfulness, care, and empathy, we can foster the internal assets and techniques expected to explore life's difficulties with elegance, insight, and flexibility.

As we go up against these normal difficulties to self-guideline, we perceive that every obstruction presents a chance for development, learning, and self-disclosure. By embracing these provocations as solicitations to develop our training and refine our abilities, we change difficulty into an open door, opening new degrees of mindfulness, strength, and close-to-home equilibrium along the way of discipline.

Developing Versatility through Self-Guideline

In the cauldron of life's hardships, flexibility arises as an encouraging sign—an unfaltering buddy that guides us through the most obscure of evenings and into the illumination of another sunrise. In this section, we investigate how becoming the best at self-guideline fills in as a strong impetus for developing flexibility and courage, notwithstanding misfortune.

At its pinnacle, flexibility is the capacity to quickly return from difficulties and disappointments with elegance, assurance, and restored force. It is a quality produced in the pot of misfortune, sharpened through the flames of battle, and tempered by the insight of involvement.

From the perspective of self-guideline, we come to comprehend how the capacity to deal with our feelings, considerations, and ways of behaving empowers us to explore life's difficulties with no sweat and versatility. By developing mindfulness, we gain understanding of our profound triggers and examples of responses, enabling us to answer affliction with serenity and clarity instead of capitulating to an incautious or receptive way of behaving.

In addition, self-guideline empowers us to keep up with viewpoints and equilibrium despite misfortune, keeping us from becoming over-powered by pressure, dread, or nervousness. By bridling the force of care, mental conduct methodologies, and unwinding procedures, we relieve our sensory system, reestablish profound balance, and develop a feeling of inward harmony and prosperity in the midst of life's tempests.

Moreover, self-guideline cultivates a feeling of organization and strengthening, empowering us to find proactive ways to adapt to misfortune, take care of issues, and adjust to evolving conditions. By rethinking difficulties as any open doors for development, learning, and self-revelation, we change misfortunes into venturing stones on the way to flexibility and individual advancement.

As we develop versatility through the act of self-guideline, we come to encapsulate the ageless insight of the peacefulness supplication—to acknowledge the things we can't change, to change the things we can, and to develop the insight to know the distinction. With every breath, every snapshot of careful mindfulness, and each demonstration of self-guideline, we fortify our ability to explore life's difficulties with effortlessness, mental fortitude, and flexibility, arising more grounded, smarter, and stronger than previously.

4

Chapter 4: Enhancing Social Awareness

Grasping social mindfulness

In the perplexing embroidery of human collaboration, social mindfulness arises as a directing compass, empowering us to explore the intricacies of associations with effortlessness, sympathy, and understanding. In this part, we leave on an excursion to disentangle the significant meaning of social mindfulness in the domain of the capacity to understand people on a deeper level.

Social mindfulness envelops the capacity to see, decipher, and answer the feelings, necessities, and viewpoints of others—aa fundamental expertise that supports significant associations, powerful correspondence, and agreeable connections. By adjusting our attention to the unobtrusive subtleties of expressive gestures, we gain knowledge of the contemplations, sentiments, and encounters of people around us, cultivating sympathy, empathy, and shared understanding.

Besides, social mindfulness fills in as a foundation for the capacity to understand people on a profound level, engaging us to explore the complexities of social elements with lucidity and knowledge. Whether in the meeting room, the study hall, or the family supper table, the capacity to peruse meaningful gestures, expect the requirements of others, and adjust our way of behaving likewise is fundamental for progress and satisfaction in all parts of life.

As we dig further into the domain of social mindfulness, we reveal useful systems and strategies for leveling up this fundamental ability. Through careful perception, undivided attention, and compassionate attunement, we develop a more profound comprehension of the rich embroidery of human experience and the manufacturing obligations of association and sympathy that rise above contrasts and join us in our common humanity.

Eventually, the excursion of upgrading social mindfulness is one of significant self-revelation and development—an excursion that welcomes us to extend our circles of sympathy, extend our associations with others, and develop a more humane and comprehensive world for all. With commitment, deliberateness, and an open heart, we set out on this extraordinary mission, realizing that the way to more noteworthy social mindfulness holds the way to opening the maximum capacity of our human connections and aggregate prosperity.

The Significance of Sympathy

At the core of social mindfulness lies sympathy—an exceptional ability to step into the shoes of another, to feel what they feel, and to see the world through their eyes. In this section, we dig into the significant meaning of sympathy in encouraging significant associations, supporting empathy, and advancing the woven artwork of human connections.

Sympathy fills in as a scaffold that rises above the obstructions of contrast, empowering us to produce profound and genuine associations with others. By adjusting our hearts to the delights and distresses, wins, and battles of people around us, we develop a sense of shared humanity that ties us together in fortitude and understanding.

Besides, compassion is a foundation of powerful correspondence, empowering us to convey warmth, understanding, and regard in our collaborations with others. Whether offering a listening ear to a companion out of luck or communicating certifiable worry for a partner's prosperity, sympathy permits us to interface on a more profound level, encouraging trust, compatibility, and shared help.

Through the act of sympathy, we develop empathy—aa significant acknowledgment of the intrinsic worth and pride of each and every person. By broadening generosity, understanding, and backing to other people, we create a gradually expanding influence of generosity and energy that elevates and enhances the existences of all who are moved by our compassion.

As we investigate the significance of sympathy in upgrading social mindfulness, we come to understand that it isn't simply an expertise to be developed but rather an approach to being—aa principal direction towards the world that shapes our collaborations, our connections, and our aggregate fate. With sympathy as our compass, we leave on an excursion of association, understanding, and shared mankind, knowing that the way to an additional sympathetic and comprehensive world starts with the straightforward demonstration of seeing and feeling humankind in one another.

Creating social capability

In the many-sided embroidery of human cooperation, social capability arises as a core value, encouraging grasping, regard, and inclusivity across different social scenes. In this part, we leave on an excursion to investigate the significant meaning of social capability in improving social mindfulness—aa fundamental part of the capacity to understand people on a deeper level that enables us to explore the intricacies of multicultural collaborations with elegance and responsiveness.

Social capability includes the capacity to comprehend, appreciate, and really draw in with people and networks from assorted social foundations. It is established with a profound regard for the extravagance and intricacy of human variety, recognizing that each culture brings its own unique points of view, values, and approaches to being to the worldwide local area.

From the perspective of social capability, we gain knowledge of the horde manners by which culture shapes our discernments, ways of behaving, and collaborations. We figure out how to perceive and regard social contrasts in correspondence styles, accepted practices, and articulations of feeling, encouraging sympathy and grasping across social partitions.

Additionally, social skills welcome us to participate in self-reflection and assessment of our own social predispositions and suppositions. By developing consciousness of our own social foundation and honors, we make space for exchange, modesty, and development, encouraging a feeling of transparency and interest in our connections with others.

As we foster social capability, we perceive that it is a continuous course of learning, development, and reflection—an excursion instead of an objective. By seeking out chances to draw in assorted viewpoints, challenge our suppositions, and extend our social familiarity, we become more powerful communicators, associates, and problem solvers in an undeniably interconnected world.

At last, the excursion of creating social capability is one of significant self-revelation and change—an excursion that welcomes us to praise the wealth and variety of human experience and to pursue fabricating a more comprehensive and evenhanded world for all. With social capability as our compass, we leave on this groundbreaking journey, realizing that the way to more noteworthy social mindfulness starts with an eagerness to embrace and gain from the intricacies of human variety.

Creating social ability

In the worldwide embroidery of human experience, social skill arises as a signal of understanding, connecting the holes between different networks and encouraging a more profound appreciation for the extravagance of human variety. This part enlightens the meaning of social skill in upgrading social mindfulness—aa basic mainstay of the capacity to understand people on a profound level that engages people to explore the intricacies of multicultural cooperation with responsiveness, regard, and compassion.

Social skills include the ability to perceive, appreciate, and actually draw in with people and gatherings from different social foundations. It requires an eagerness to suspend judgment, challenge suppositions, and move toward social experiences with interest and modesty. By developing social skills, people gain a more profound comprehension of the special qualities, standards, and customs that shape the lived encounters of others, encouraging a feeling of association and having a place across social partitions.

Vital to the improvement of social skills is the acknowledgment of one's own social focal point and the inclinations that might vary one's insights and cooperation. Through thoughtfulness and self-reflection, people can uncover oblivious inclinations and suspicions, permitting them to draw in social contrasts with more prominent receptiveness and awareness.

In addition, social skill involves the capacity to adjust one's correspondence style, conduct, and perspective to accommodate a variety of social standards and assumptions. By embracing adaptability and flexibility, people can explore social experiences effortlessly, encouraging trust, shared regard, and viable correspondence.

As people develop their social skills, they become better prepared to explore the intricacies of multicultural cooperation in various settings, whether in the working environment, instructive foundations, or local area spaces. By encouraging a climate of inclusivity and regard, social capability lays the groundwork for significant exchange, coordinated effort, and social change.

At last, the excursion of creating social skills is one of nonstop mastering, development, and self-disclosure—an excursion that welcomes people to extend their points of view, challenge their suspicions, and commend the magnificence of human variety. With social capability as a core value, people can produce further associations, cultivate shared understanding, and make a more comprehensive and evenhanded world for all.

Leveling up nonverbal correspondence abilities

In the complex dance of human collaboration, nonverbal correspondence arises as a quiet ensemble, passing on an abundance of data and significance beyond the limits of words. This section investigates the significance of leveling up nonverbal correspondence abilities in improving social mindfulness—aa basic part of the capacity to understand people on a deeper level that empowers people to decipher and answer the unobtrusive prompts and signals that shape relational elements.

Nonverbal correspondence incorporates a large number of signs, including looks, non-verbal communication, motions, stances, and manners of speaking. These nonverbal signs give important insights into the feelings, expectations, and perspectives of others, permitting people to recognize fundamental implications and explore social co-operation with more prominent clarity and awareness.

By improving their nonverbal correspondence abilities, people can upgrade their capacity to convey sympathy, warmth, and grasping in their associations with others. Through cognizant attention to their own nonverbal signals and the capacity to decipher those of others, people can encourage compatibility, assemble trust, and develop further associations in both individual and expert connections.

Besides, nonverbal correspondence assumes an essential role in laying out friendly limits, conveying regard, and working with common understanding. By focusing on inconspicuous signals, for example, eye-to-eye connection, looks, and body pose, people can explore social collaborations with more noteworthy artfulness, guaranteeing that their correspondence is both successful and aware of others' limits and inclinations.

As people foster their nonverbal relational abilities, they become more adept at perusing the inconspicuous subtleties of social connections and adjusting their way of behaving appropriately. Whether in conventional settings like conferences or casual settings like parties, improving nonverbal correspondence abilities empowers people to speak with legitimacy, clarity, and responsiveness, cultivating amicable connections and shared understanding.

Rehearsing undivided attention

In the orchestra of human association, undivided attention arises as an amicable tune—aa song that resounds with sympathy, understanding, and veritable commitment. This section digs into the extraordinary force of undivided attention in upgrading social mindfulness, a foundation of the capacity to understand people on a profound level that cultivates profound associations, shared regard, and successful correspondence.

Undivided attention is something other than hearing words; it is a unique way of completely captivating someone else's considerations, sentiments, and encounters. It includes really focusing, suspending judgment, and showing certifiable interest in what the speaker needs to say. Through undivided attention, we create a protected and steady space for others to put themselves out there genuinely, encouraging trust, compatibility, and shared understanding.

Key to the act of undivided attention is the development of sympathy—the capacity to step into someone else's point of view and see the world according to their viewpoint. By relating to the speaker's feelings and encounters, we exhibit empathy and approval, sustaining a feeling of association and having a place that rises above words alone.

In addition, undivided attention includes dynamic commitment and support in the discussion, including posing unassuming inquiries, summarizing, and giving criticism. By effectively taking part in the discourse, we exhibit our veritable interest in grasping the speaker's point of view, cultivating further associations, and working with common comprehension.

As people practice undivided attention, they foster a more prominent appreciation for the extravagance and variety of human encounters, points of view, and feelings. Whether in private connections, proficient settings, or local area associations, undivided attention empowers people to produce further associations, resolve clashes, and team up more successfully towards shared objectives.

Eventually, the excursion of rehearsing undivided attention is one of developing compassion, encouraging association, and sustaining shared regard—an excursion that improves our lives and fortifies the texture of our networks. With undivided attention as a core value, people can develop more noteworthy social mindfulness, upgrade their capacity to understand individuals on a profound level, and contribute to a more caring and comprehensive world for all.

5

Chapter 5: Nurturing Relationship Management

Building Trust and Affinity

In the perplexing dance of human connections, trust and affinity arise as primary points of support, whereupon the structure of association and closeness is fabricated. This section digs into the significant meaning of trust and compatibility in supporting powerful relationships among executives—aa foundation of the capacity to understand people on a profound level that encourages realness, shared regard, and flexibility in relational collaborations.

Trust is the bedrock of solid connections, enveloping a feeling of unwavering quality, honesty, and profound wellbeing that permits people to have a real sense of reassurance and feel weak in one another's presence. Compatibility, then again, alludes to the feeling of association, understanding, and common proclivity that emerges when people share normal interests, values, and encounters. Together, trust and compatibility structure the bedrock of sound, satisfying connections, laying the strong groundwork on which more profound associations can prosper.

Building trust and compatibility requires purposeful exertion, tolerance, and compassion. It includes showing consistency, straightforwardness, and respectability in a way that would sound natural to one and their activities, encouraging a climate of security and realness where people go ahead and put themselves out there transparently and truly. By effectively tuning in, approving feelings, and showing veritable interest in others' encounters, people can manufacture further associations and develop significant connections in light of trust and common regard.

Besides, building trust and compatibility includes sustaining a sense of mutual perspective and shared objectives, cultivating joint effort, and participating in the quest for shared goals. By adjusting values, dreams, and desires, people can fortify their bonds, develop their associations, and work together towards a more brilliant, seriously satisfying future.

As people develop trust and affinity in their connections, they establish the groundwork for more profound closeness, understanding, and association. Whether in private connections, proficient joint efforts, or local area commitment, trust and compatibility act as core values that encourage flexibility, sympathy, and common help, improving the texture of human cooperation and adding to a more empathetic and agreeable world for all.

Powerful relational abilities

In the complicated embroidered artwork of human cooperation, correspondence fills in as the energetic string that winds around the texture of connections, interfacing hearts and psyches with the sensitive strands of words, motions, and articulations. This part dives into the fundamental job of compelling relational abilities in sustaining relationships—aa foundation of the capacity to understand people on a profound level that enables people to communicate their thoughts genuinely, interface with others profoundly, and explore the intricacies of relational elements with elegance and lucidity.

Viable correspondence is something other than passing on data; it is a unique course of common trade and understanding that requires undivided attention, sympathy, and lucidity of articulation. It includes the craft of articulating one's contemplations, sentiments, and necessities with genuineness and credibility while additionally taking care of the points of view, feelings, and encounters of others.

At the core of powerful correspondence lies undivided attention—an act of concentrating entirely on the speaker, suspending judgment, and looking to grasp their point of view with compassion and receptiveness. Through undivided attention, people show regard, approval, and compassion, encouraging a feeling of trust and compatibility that lays the groundwork for solid, satisfying connections.

In addition, powerful correspondence envelops the capacity to communicate one's thoughts confidently and with certainty while likewise regarding the limits and needs of others. It includes the talented route of relational struggles, conflicts, and false impressions with sympathy, strategy, and versatility.

By leveling up their correspondence abilities, people can develop further associations, resolve clashes valuably, and encourage a culture of transparency and joint effort in their connections. Whether in private cooperations, proficient joint efforts, or local area commitment, viable correspondence fills in as an impetus for development, understanding, and shared regard, enhancing the texture of human association and adding to a more agreeable and interconnected world for all.

Compromise Procedures

In the embroidery of human connections, struggle arises as a characteristic and unavoidable part of relational elements—aa string woven into the texture of association and closeness, provoking us to explore contrasts with effortlessness, empathy, and strength. This part dives into the intricacies of compromise in relationships—an essential part of the capacity to understand people on a profound level that engages people to address conflicts helpfully, save trust, and fortify the obligations of association.

Struggle, however frequently seen from a perspective of uneasiness or difficulty, presents a chance for development, understanding, and change. When drawn closer with transparency, sympathy, and a pledge to common regard, struggle can act as an impetus for more profound closeness, more clear correspondence, and reinforced obligations of trust.

Viable compromise requires a diverse methodology, incorporating systems for de-raising strains, encouraging comprehension, and tracking down commonly gainful arrangements. It includes the development of sympathy, undivided attention, and confidence, empowering people to communicate their requirements and worries while likewise taking care of the viewpoints and feelings of others.

One vital technique in compromise will be splitting the difference—aa readiness to meet midway, investigate shared conviction, and look for arrangements that honor the necessities and interests of all gatherings included. By encouraging a feeling of coordinated effort and participation, people can explore conflicts with compassion and understanding, saving the respectability of their connections while likewise tracking down solutions to clashes.

Furthermore, exchange abilities assume a critical role in compromise, enabling people to investigate effective fixes, conceptualize options, and find mutually beneficial results that address the basic requirements and interests of the two players. Through successful exchange, people can change struggle into a chance for development, learning, and more profound association.

Eventually, compromise is a dynamic and progressing process—an excursion of investigation, correspondence, and compromise that welcomes people to incline toward uneasiness with boldness and empathy. By embracing struggle as a characteristic and unavoidable part of connections, people can develop versatility, reinforce their bonds, and encourage a culture of understanding and common regard in their collaborations.

Close to home guidelines in Connections

Inside the perplexing dance of human connections, feelings undergo rhythmic movement like the tides, forming the shapes of our communications and shading the scene of our associations. This section investigates the critical role of profound guidelines in relationships for executives—aa foundation of the capacity to understand people on a deeper level that enables people to explore the intricacies of relational elements with beauty, sympathy, and flexibility.

Profound guidelines include cognizant mindfulness and the board of one's own feelings because of outer improvements or inside triggers. It is the capacity to perceive and balance the power and articulation of one's feelings, considering helpful commitment and successful correspondence in connections.

With regards to connections, the close-to-home guideline fills in as a directing compass, empowering people to answer testing circumstances with lucidity, sympathy, and understanding. It includes the development of mindfulness—the capacity to perceive and mark one's feelings—as well as the advancement of survival methods and unwinding procedures to deal with close-to-home excitement and keep calm in troublesome conditions.

Moreover, profound guidelines envelop the limit with regards to sympathy—the capacity to adjust to the feelings and encounters of others with empathy and understanding. By understanding the sentiments and viewpoints of our accomplices, companions, or associates, we encourage further associations and reinforce the obligations of trust and closeness in our connections.

Compelling close-to-home guidelines additionally include defining limits and discussing them decisively with others, guaranteeing that our own requirements and feelings are regarded and respected with regards to the relationship. By communicating our thoughts really and emphatically while likewise taking care of the feelings and necessities of others, we create an underpinning of shared regard and understanding that supports sound, satisfying connections.

As people develop close-to-home guidelines in their connections, they prepare for more profound closeness, more clear correspondence, and more prominent flexibility, notwithstanding challenges. By saddling the force of the ability to understand anyone on a profound level to explore the ups and downs of human association with beauty and sympathy, people can develop connections that are feeding, steady, and profoundly satisfying.

Developing Sympathy and Empathy

In the huge woven artwork of human connections, sympathy and empathy arise as directing stars, enlightening the way towards more profound association, understanding, and shared help. This part investigates the extraordinary force of sympathy and empathy in relationships among executives—aa foundation of the capacity to understand people on a deeper level that encourages compassion, understanding, and flexibility in relational cooperation.

Sympathy is the capacity to step into someone else's point of view, to see and grasp their feelings, encounters, and points of view with responsiveness and empathy. The extension interfaces hearts and psyches, rising above contrasts and encouraging a significant feeling of association and having a place.

Sympathy, then again, is the ardent longing to reduce the suffering of others and to act with thoughtfulness and liberality towards those out of luck. It is the main impetus behind thoughtful gestures, sympathy, and backing, supporting the obligations of association, and cultivating a sense of local area and fortitude.

Together, sympathy and empathy structure the bedrock of sound, satisfying connections, giving a system to common figuring out, backing, and development. By developing compassion, people can adjust to the feelings and encounters of others, encouraging further associations and reinforcing the obligations of trust and closeness in their connections.

Besides, empathy empowers people to answer the necessities and endure others with benevolence and liberality, creating a culture of care and support that supports sound, lively connections. Whether through thoughtful gestures, uplifting statements, or essentially listening carefully, empathy sustains a feeling of association and having a place, encouraging versatility and prosperity despite life's difficulties.

As people develop sympathy and empathy in their connections, they encourage a culture of figuring out, support, and shared regard that improves the texture of human association. By encapsulating the standards of sympathy and empathy in their cooperation with others, people can make connections that are feeding, steady, and profoundly satisfying, adding to a more empathetic and agreeable world for all.

6

Chapter 6: Putting It All Together

Incorporation of Abilities

As we venture through the complexities of the capacity to understand people on a deeper level, we come to understand that every expertise we've investigated from top to bottom—whether it's mindfulness, self-guideline, social mindfulness, or relationship management—is definitely not a secluded island but instead interconnected features of an all-encompassing system. In this last part, we center around the reconciliation of these abilities, perceiving that their collaboration is where the genuine force of the capacity to appreciate people on a deeper level lies.

Reconciliation implies uniting every one of the devices and bits of knowledge we've accumulated enroute and meshing them into the texture of our day-to-day routines. It's tied in with applying mindfulness to perceive our profound triggers, using self-guideline methods to deal with our reactions, utilizing social attention to figure out others' viewpoints, and utilizing relationships' abilities to encourage solid associations.

Through coordination, we make an agreeable stream—aa dance of mindfulness and sympathy, credibility and empathy—that directs our collaborations with ourselves as well as other people. Coordination empowers us to explore life's intricacies with elegance and strength, answering difficulties with clarity and empathy as opposed to responding imprudently or protectively.

To outline this mix, we dig into genuine situations, showing how people apply the capacity to understand anyone at their core abilities in different settings. From the meeting room to the homeroom, from the family supper table to the local gathering, we witness the groundbreaking effect of the capacity to appreciate people on a profound level in real life, encouraging figuring out, joint effort, and positive results.

Also, we offer viable activities and exercises to assist perusers with integrating these abilities into their own lives. These activities open doors to reflection, practice, and development, enabling perusers to extend how they might interpret themselves as well as other people and to apply the ability to understand anyone on a deeper level in significant ways.

At last, mix is tied in with exemplifying the standards of the capacity to appreciate people on a profound level in our viewpoints, words, and activities, both exclusively and all in all. As we integrate these abilities into our lives, we not only upgrade our own prosperity and connections but additionally add to a more humane, sympathetic, and amicable world for all.

Contextual analyses and models

In the mosaic of human experience, stories act as windows into the lived truth of the capacity to understand people on a profound level in real life. In this section, we dig into convincing contextual analyses and striking models that enlighten the extraordinary force of the ability to appreciate anyone on a profound level across different settings and situations.

Through these contextual analyses and models, we witness the utilization of the capacity to appreciate people on a profound level, in actuality, in circumstances ranging from the everyday to the unprecedented. We notice people exploring complex relational elements, overseeing struggle with elegance and strength, and encouraging pro-found associations in light of trust, compassion, and understanding.

One such model might portray a group chief in a corporate setting who, through mindfulness and sympathy, perceives the extraordinary qualities and difficulties of each colleague, cultivating a culture of cooperation and development. Another model could feature a parent-youngster relationship, where viable correspondence and profound guidelines empower the two players to explore clashes with compassion and common regard.

By looking at these contextual analyses and models, perusers gain knowledge into the pragmatic utilization of the ability to understand anyone on a deeper level of abilities in their regular day-to-day existence. They perceive how mindfulness can prompt more noteworthy genuineness and self-acknowledgment, how self-guideline can diffuse tense circumstances and advance close-to-home prosperity, how social mindfulness can cultivate compassion and inclusivity, and how relationships can sustain further associations and flexibility.

In addition, these contextual analyses and models act as motivation and inspiration for perusers on their own excursion of the ability to appreciate people on a profound level. They exhibit that the capacity to understand people on a profound level is certainly not a theoretical idea but rather a substantial arrangement of abilities that can be developed and applied to enhance our lives and connections.

As perusers draw in with these contextual analyses and models, they are urged to ponder their own encounters and consider how they could apply the standards of the ability to appreciate people on a deeper level in their own lives. Through this course of reflection and investigation, perusers extend how they might interpret the ability to appreciate people on a deeper level and its extraordinary potential, making ready for self-improvement, significant associations, and positive change.

Useful Activities

In the pursuit of dominating ability to understand anyone on a pro-found level, hypothesis alone is deficient. Reasonable application is the cauldron where information changes into shrewdness and abilities are sharpened through conscious practice. This section presents an assortment of reasonable activities intended to engage perusers to apply the standards of the capacity to understand people on a profound level in their day-to-day routines.

These activities offer an involved way to deal with extending mindfulness, improving self-guideline, developing social mindfulness, and refining relationship skills. They give valuable open doors to reflection, contemplation, and trial and error, directing perusers on an excursion of self-disclosure and development.

For example, one activity might incite perusers to keep a day-to-day diary of their feelings, contemplations, and responses, encouraging mindfulness and care. Another activity could include rehearsing profound breathing or care contemplation to develop self-guideline and close-to-home flexibility.

Essentially, practices zeroed in on friendly mindfulness might include rehearsing undivided attention abilities in discussions with companions or relatives or participating in context-taking activities to grasp others' perspectives and encounters.

Also, in practices connected with relationships, the board might incorporate pretend situations to rehearse emphatic correspondence or compromise strategies, or participate in thoughtful gestures and sympathy to sustain connections and assemble trust.

These useful activities are not intended to be one-size-fits-all arrangements, but rather versatile devices that perusers can design to their own necessities, inclinations, and conditions. They energize trial and error and self-disclosure, engaging perusers to create a customized tool compartment with the capacity to understand people on a profound level through techniques that impact them.

By drawing in with these down-to-earth works, perusers extend how they might interpret the capacity to appreciate anyone on a deeper level and gain trust in their capacity to apply these abilities, all things considered, in all circumstances. They become dynamic members in their own development and advancement, opening the groundbreaking capability of the ability to appreciate people on a profound level to improve their lives and connections.

Reflection and self-appraisal

Chasing dominating ability to understand anyone on a profound level, thoughtfulness, and self-evaluation act as directing reference points, enlightening the way to self-revelation and development. This section urges perusers to take part in all things considered and self-evaluation, welcoming them to extend how they might interpret their own capacity to understand people on a profound level and recognize regions for additional turns of events.

Reflection includes taking a step back from the hecticness of our day-to-day existence to consider our contemplations, sentiments, and activities with interest and transparency. Through reflection, we gain knowledge about our assets and shortcomings, examples of conduct, and hidden convictions and values. We likewise have the potential to analyze previous encounters and gain from both our triumphs and disappointments, preparing for self-awareness and change.

Self-appraisal, then again, includes deliberately assessing our ability to understand anyone on a profound level of abilities and skills. It might include finishing self-evaluation surveys or tests to measure our degree of mindfulness, self-guideline, social mindfulness, and relation-ship with the board. By evaluating our capacity to understand people on a deeper level in an organized and objective way, we gain clarity on regions where we succeed and regions where we might have to concentrate our endeavors.

Through reflection and self-appraisal, perusers extend how they might interpret their own ability to understand anyone on a deeper level and gain significant bits of knowledge into regions for develop-ment and improvement. They become more mindful of their assets and shortcomings, empowering them to settle on informed conclusions about how to best use their assets and address regions for development.

Besides, reflection and self-evaluation encourage a feeling of organi-zation and strengthening, engaging perusers to take responsibility for the capacity to understand people on a profound level. They become dynamic members in their own development and advancement, focused on developing the abilities and skills that will empower them to flourish in their own and proficient lives.

By taking part in truth-telling and self-appraisal, perusers lay the groundwork for further development and change in their capacity to understand anyone on a profound level. They become more sensitive to their viewpoints, sentiments, and ways of behaving and better prepared to explore the intricacies of human associations with effortlessness, sympathy, and credibility.

Making an Individual Activity Plan

As we arrive at the climax of our investigation into the capacity to understand individuals on a deeper level, we take an urgent step towards enduring change and development: making an individual activity plan. This section guides perusers in making a guide for their continuous excursion of the capacity to understand people on a deeper level of events, illustrating explicit objectives, systems, and responsibility measures to help their advancement.

An individual activity plan starts with a reflection on the experiences acquired all through the book—the qualities found, the difficulties recognized, and the desires imagined. From this establishment, perusers are urged to set explicit, quantifiable, feasible, applicable, and time-bound (Brilliant) objectives that line up with their qualities and yearnings.

These objectives might incorporate different parts of the ability to appreciate people at their core, for example, upgrading mindfulness, working on self-guideline, extending social mindfulness, or refining relationship skills. Every objective ought to be joined by substantial activity steps and a timetable for completion, guaranteeing lucidity and concentration while chasing development and improvement.

Besides, the individual activity plan incorporates methodologies for beating deterrents and misfortunes, as well as ways of commending accomplishments and achievements enroute. It likewise incorporates instruments for responsibility, like imparting objectives to a confided-in companion or tutor, or following advancement through journaling or self-evaluation devices.

By making an individual activity plan, perusers focus on their continuous development and improvement in capacity to understand people on a profound level. They become designers of their own prosperity, engaged in developing the abilities and skills that will empower them to explore life's difficulties with flexibility, sympathy, and validity.

As perusers set out on their own activity plans, they become problem solvers in their own daily routines as well as in the lives of people around them. Through their obligation to have the capacity to understand individuals on a deeper level, they contribute to a more sympathetic, compassionate, and amicable world for all.